Amazing Animals
Fishes

Please visit our web site at www.garethstevens.com
For a free catalog describing our list of high-quality books, call 1-800-542-2595 (USA) or 1-800-387-3178 (Canada).
Our fax: 1-877-542-2596

Library of Congress Cataloging-in-Publication Data

Barnard, Edward S.
    Fishes / by Edward S. Barnard.
            p. cm.—(Amazing Animals)
          Originally published: Pleasantville, NY: Reader's Digest Young Families, 2007.
          Includes bibliographical references and index.
          ISBN-10: 0-8368-9106-6 ISBN-13: 978-0-8368-9106-5 (lib. bdg.)
          ISBN-10: 1-4339-2023-9 ISBN-13: 978-1-4339-2023-3 (soft cover)
    1. Fishes—Juvenile literature. I. Title.
    QL617.2.B37 2009
    597—dc22   2008027901

This edition first published in 2009 by
Gareth Stevens Publishing
A Weekly Reader® Company
1 Reader's Digest Road
Pleasantville, NY 10570-7000 USA

This edition copyright © 2009 by Gareth Stevens, Inc. Original edition copyright © 2007 by Reader's Digest Young Families,
Pleasantville, NY 10570

Gareth Stevens Senior Managing Editor: Lisa M. Herrington
Gareth Stevens Creative Director: Lisa Donovan
Gareth Stevens Art Director: Ken Crossland
Gareth Stevens Associate Editor: Amanda Hudson
Gareth Stevens Publisher: Keith Garton

Consultant: Robert E. Budliger (Retired), NY State Department of Environmental Conservation

Photo Credits
Front cover: Dreamstime.com/Tommy Schultz, Title page: JupiterImages, Contents page: iStockphoto.com/Gabriel Eckert, pages 6-7: JupiterImages,
page 8: U.S. Fish and Wildlife Service, page 10: U.S. Fish and Wildlife Service, page 11: Dreamstime.com/LightArt, pages 12 and 13: U.S. Fish and
Wildlife Service, pages 14-15: Dreamstime.com/Ian Scott, page 16: iStockphoto.com/Keith Flood, page 17: LadyofHats, page 18: iStockphoto.
com/Dan Schmitt, page 19: iStockphoto.com/Ian Stock, page 20: JupiterImages, pages 22-23: Corel Corporation, page 24: iStockphoto.com/Heike
Loos, page 25: Dreamstime.com/Yuri Arcurs, page 26: Dreamstime.com/Loren Rodgers, page 27: Wendy Rathey/Creative Commons, page 28:
iStockphoto.com/Dejan Sarman, page 29: chai kian shin/Shutterstock Inc., pages 30-31: iStockphoto.com/Wolfgang Amri, page 32: iStockphoto.
com/Luan Tran, page 33: janderk, page 34: Fred Hsu/Monterey Bay Aquarium, California, page 35: iStockphoto.com/Harald Bolten, page 36:
Edward S. Barnard, page 37: ValueClips Clip Art/Unlisted Images, Inc., pages 38-39: iStockphoto.com/Dennis Sabo, page 40: iStockphoto.com/
Dieter Spears, page 42: Dreamstime.com/Kathy Wynn, page 43: Danilo Cedrone/Courtesy of United Nations Food and Agriculture Organization,
pages 44-45: iStockphoto.com/Boris Tarasov, Back cover: Dreamstime.com/Lynette Lee hwee ling.

Printed in the United States of America

1 2 3 4 5 6 7 8 9 13 12 11 10 09

Amazing Animals
Fishes

By Edward S. Barnard

Gareth Stevens
Publishing

Contents

Chapter 1
A Salmon Story

Sockeye salmon change color only after they leave the ocean and enter a river. Their silvery, black-spotted sides turn red while their shiny heads and tails become green.

Fish or Fishes?

When you are talking about two or more of the same kind of fish, use the word **fish**. When you mean different kinds of fishes, use **fishes**.

It is July in the Pacific Ocean. A **school** of sockeye salmon is heading toward the west coast of Canada. More than two years ago, these fish were born in a stream miles from the coast. They made their way to the ocean as small fish. They have been far out in the Pacific ever since.

The school is swimming hard, not even stopping to eat as it reaches the river. The salmon taste the familiar flavor of their home stream. They know they must swim up this river, to reach the place where they were born.

Once the salmon leave the ocean, changes take place in their bodies that allow them to switch from living in saltwater to living in freshwater (water that is not salty).

By September, the salmon school is many miles up the river. Hundreds of fish have died along the way, but thousands have survived. In October, they reach a lake. When they were young, the salmon spent a year or two in this lake before going to the ocean. They cannot stay here now.

The salmon must swim to the spot where their home stream runs into the lake. They head up the narrow, quick-flowing stream to the same place they were born. Males take the lead. Females follow.

When a female arrives at her birthplace, she finds a male salmon already there. She scoops out a hollow in the stream's pebbly bottom with her tail. As she begins laying her eggs, the male swims along to fertilize them. Then the female scoops out another nest. The sand or mud she scoops out from this nest covers the eggs in the first nest and keeps them safe. The pair repeats this process up to seven times. By the end, the female has laid as many as four thousand eggs!

A week or two later, all the adult salmon die. But inside the eggs, baby salmon are growing. By mid-December, eyes begin to appear in each pink egg.

Ready to Hatch

Each round salmon egg is no bigger than the eraser on a pencil. You can see the eyes of the baby salmon inside the eggs about a month after the eggs are laid.

Streams filled with salmon swimming to their nests can be very crowded. Males often fight over nesting space.

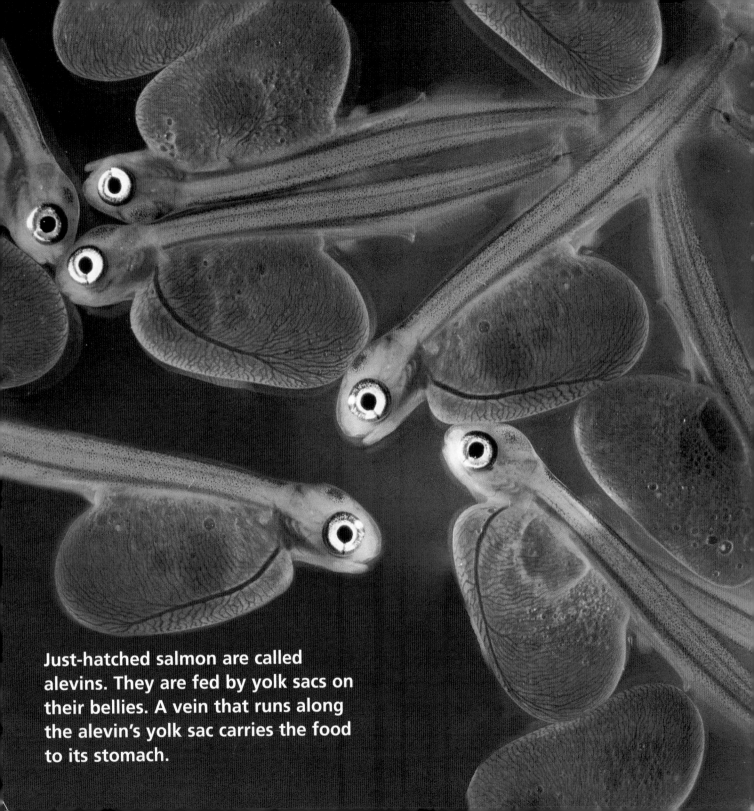

Just-hatched salmon are called alevins. They are fed by yolk sacs on their bellies. A vein that runs along the alevin's yolk sac carries the food to its stomach.

In late winter, tiny salmon called alevins (AL eh venz) wriggle out of the eggs into the stream's cold water. They have huge eyes and orange yolk sacs that provide food.

The alevins hide in the pebbles for three or four months. Then they lose their orange yolk sacs. They swim up from the stream bottom as tiny greenish-brown fish with black spots called fry. The fry swim downstream to the lake.

The fry spend the next year or two in the lake. They grow larger, and their bodies change so that they can live in saltwater. Now they are silvery, medium-size fish known as smolts. From the lake, they swim down a river to the sea. In about two years, they will come back to the very same stream to create the next generation of sockeye salmon.

Sockeye Salmon Life Stages

When a sockeye salmon starts life, it is called an alevin. When it begins to swim, it is called a fry. When it is ready to enter the ocean, it is called a smolt. While in the ocean, sockeye salmon are silver. After they leave the ocean for a river, they turn red and green.

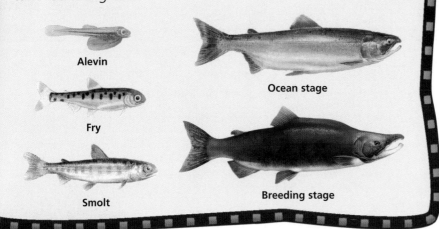

Alevin

Fry

Smolt

Ocean stage

Breeding stage

Chapter 2
The Body of a Fish

A great white shark cruises slowly above a school of small fish. A great white shark can swim as fast as 35 miles (56 kilometers) an hour for short distances—seven times faster than an Olympic swimmer!

What Is a Fish?

A fish is an animal with a backbone, fins, and **gills** that lives in water. A fish sucks in water through its mouth and pushes it out through **gill slits** behind its head. **Oxygen**, a gas all animals need to live, passes from the water through the gills and into the fish's blood. Most fishes are **cold-blooded**. Their body temperature is usually the same as the water around them.

Three Kinds of Fishes

There are three main groups of fishes—bony fishes, sharks and rays, and jawless fishes. Bony fishes have hard skeletons made of bone. Sharks and rays have flexible skeletons made of **cartilage**, which is similar to the material that forms our ears and noses. Jawless fishes also have skeletons made of cartilage, but instead of jaws they have suckerlike mouths with small teeth.

No Jaws, No Problem

Jawless fishes, such as lampreys, attach themselves to other fishes with their sucking mouths and eat into the flesh of their **prey**.

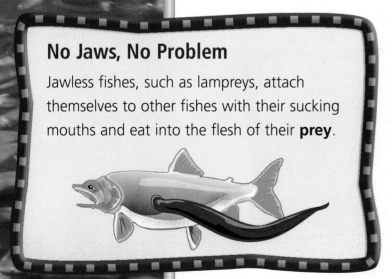

Moving in the Water

Most fishes have streamlined bodies that help them slip easily through water. But the shapes of the bodies are very different. Tunas are shaped like teardrops. Eels are long and thin like snakes. Flounders are flat like pancakes.

A typical fish swims by wiggling the rear part of its body and tail from side to side. It curves its body into a S shape with its muscles. A fish moves its fins to hold itself steady, to turn, and to stop.

To change depth, a bony fish uses a sac filled with air inside its body called a **swim bladder**. To go up, the fish lets more air into the swim bladder. To go down, it lets air out.

Waiting for a Meal

Moray eels hide in nooks and crannies of coral reefs, waiting for smaller fishes to swim by. Then the eels dart out and grab their prey with strong jaws lined with needle-sharp teeth.

Rays swim by slowly waving their large triangular fins up and down. This eagle ray is a gentle creature and will use the poisonous stinger at the end of its thin tail only if attacked.

The grouper's mouth and gills are so powerful that the grouper can suck in small fish from a distance.

Fish Senses

A fish has wide vision. It can see on both sides of its head, behind, and in front—all at the same time!

A fish has ears, but they are inside the fish's head, behind the eyes. Sounds travel very well through water and easily enter a fish's body. Fishes use sounds to attract mates and to warn off rivals.

A fish smells using nostrils located on the sides of its head. Some sharks can detect one drop of blood in an Olympic-size swimming pool!

A fish has **taste buds** in its mouth. Some fishes also have taste buds on the outside of their heads and fins. Catfish have taste buds on their whiskerlike feelers.

Nerve Lineup

A fish has nerves that form a line along each side of its body. This line is called a **lateral line**. The nerves detect tiny differences in pressure around the fish. Lateral lines help fishes swim close together in schools without bumping into one another.

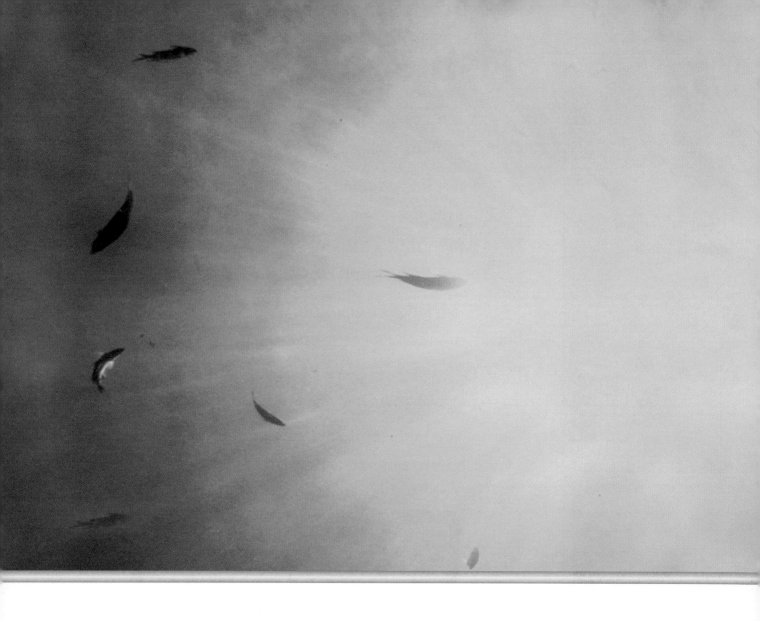

Chapter 3
Surviving Underwater

Blue-striped grunts swim in schools at night but do not bump into each other.

School Time

Fishes often swim in large groups of hundreds or thousands. These groups are called schools. Swimming in a school gives each fish extra protection. It is less likely that one fish will be attacked when it has other fish around it. Also, a school of fish has more eyes to spot **predators**.

With more eyes looking for food, fishes in schools can find more to eat and feed on larger kinds of foods than if they were swimming alone.

Fishes use less energy when they swim in groups. This is because a fish creates water currents when it swims, giving a boost to others next to it.

No School!

Some fishes that live on the bottom of a lake, river, or ocean don't swim in schools. They live alone, like this frogfish. It wiggles the lure above its mouth to attract prey.

Baby Fishes

Most female fishes lay hundreds or thousands of eggs in the water, where they are fertilized by males. The eggs range in size from tiny specks to pea-sized blobs. When the eggs hatch, the newborn fish are usually on their own. Only a few survive to become adults.

Some female fishes, such as sharks, give birth to a few young at a time. The babies look like tiny sharks.

Some fishes care for their eggs. Sunfish scoop out nests on pond bottoms and protect their eggs. Female seahorses lay their eggs in special pockets on males called brood pouches. Female African cichlids (SIK leds) carry their eggs in their mouths. After the babies hatch, mothers keep them in their mouths for several weeks.

Eggs in the Sand

Grunion are small fish that live along the California coast. On certain spring nights during high tides, they leave the water to lay and fertilize their eggs on sandy beaches. The sand keeps the eggs warm. During the next high tides, about two weeks later, the baby grunion hatch and are carried out to sea by the waves.

The leafy sea dragon looks a lot like the leafy seaweed around it. This helps the fish hide from predators. Females lay their eggs on the males' tails. The males carry the eggs until the young hatch.

Two remoras save energy by taking a ride on a sea turtle. The remoras will try to catch leftover bits of the turtle's meals.

remoras

Finding Food

Most fishes eat other animals and compete with each other for food. Some fishes, such as tunas and great white sharks, just swim through the water looking for prey.

Other fishes have special ways of feeding. Remoras, also known as suckerfish, attach themselves to larger fishes and turtles using a sucking disc on the top of their heads. When their hosts eat, the remoras catch the leftover scraps. Little fishes called cleaners feed on the dead skin and the tiny creatures that live on other fishes. These other fishes sometimes line up as they wait to be cleaned. Large fishes even let the cleaners enter their mouths and clean their gills.

A few fishes have very unusual ways of getting their food. The electric eel of South America kills or stuns its prey just by touching it! The eel's muscles produce an electric current.

All Puffed Up

A porcupine fish sucks in water and makes itself three times its normal size when a predator comes near. As the porcupine fish puffs up, spines on its skin stick straight out. This makes the fish too spiky to eat!

Chapter 4
Ocean Fishes

A trumpet fish waits for small fishes to come close enough to grab. It won't try to eat one of the pink squirrel fish, though. They are too big and have poisonous spines on their fins.

trumpet fish

Coral Reef Fishes

Coral reefs can be found in the shallow waters of the tropics. The reefs are filled with hiding spaces. Many different fishes and other animals live in coral reefs.

Some reef fishes form schools and feed on tiny living things in the water. Some eat the soft parts of the corals. Some crack open snails and sea urchins. Some larger fishes, such as barracudas and sharks, stalk smaller fishes.

Most reef fishes are very colorful. They use colors and patterns to attract mates, warn other fishes away from their territories, and blend into colorful backgrounds.

Natural Protection

Clownfish never swim far from sea anemones, creatures with stinging tentacles that attach themselves to rocks or coral reefs. Clownfish are the only fishes not affected by the anemones' poison. Without an anemone's protection, a clownfish would soon be eaten.

Top Ocean Fishes

There are no hiding places in the upper layers of the open ocean. But many fishes that live there can be hard to see. From above, their blue or gray backs blend in with the color of the water. Looking from below, their silver or white undersides blend in with the sunlight.

Some fishes of the open ocean, such as tunas, are fast. They speed through the water, eating smaller fishes. But the two largest ocean fishes are slow. The whale shark, the biggest fish of all, is as long and heavy as a school bus. It swims very slowly, eating only tiny creatures. It strains them from the water with hairy bristles in its mouth.

The ocean sunfish, the largest bony fish, can grow to be 10 feet (3 meters) long. It swims even more slowly than the whale shark. It spends much of its time at the surface. There it lets seabirds pick tiny creatures off its body.

Ocean sunfish

The whale shark's upper body is mostly gray with rows of yellow spots. The exact arrangement of these spots is different on each whale shark!

Live From the Deep!

The coelacanth (SEE luh kanth) was a fish that lived at least 400 million years ago. Scientists know this from fossils showing the fish's skeleton. They thought the fish was extinct. But in the 1930s and again in the 1990s, living coelacanths were discovered deep in the Indian Ocean!

Down in the dark, deep sea are thousands of unusual fishes. Some have glow-in-the-dark lights!

Weird Fishes of the Deep.

Only the top 1,500 feet (457 m) of the ocean gets any sunlight. It is inky black below this point, which stretches down 10,000 feet to 15,000 feet (3,048 to 4,572 m). If you imagine icing on a cake, you'll have a good idea of how thin the sunlight part of the ocean is compared to its total depth.

Many fishes living in this dark world are black with spots that glow in the dark. They feed on shrimps and other fishes attracted to their lights. Each kind of glowing fish has its own pattern of lights. These patterns may help fishes find each other to form schools.

Deep-sea fish called anglerfish wiggle glowing lures from stalks on their heads to attract prey. Other fishes known as gulpers or pelican eels have big jaws and can swallow prey their own size or larger.

Chapter 5
Worlds of Water

The largemouth bass of North American ponds and lakes puts up a good fight when it is hooked!

Freshwater Fishes

Scientists have identified about 25,000 different kinds of fishes. About 10,000 of these live in freshwater at least part of their lives.

Freshwater fishes such as trout and salmon live in cool lakes and streams. Other fishes such as perch, bass, and pickerel swim in slower-moving rivers and lakes where water plants hide their food—minnows, frogs, and insects.

Catfish have feelers around their mouths that help them find food in muddy water at the bottom of lakes, rivers, and ponds. Catfish can live in water that is too warm and polluted for most other fishes.

Many freshwater fishes are in danger of becoming extinct. They are threatened by pollution and other human activities.

Biggest Catch Ever
The largest freshwater fish on record is a Mekong River catfish caught in Thailand. It weighed 646 pounds (293 kilograms)!

Endangered Ocean Fishes

The giant bluefin tuna can grow to be 12 feet (3.6 m) long, weigh up to 1,500 pounds (680 kg), and live as long as 30 years. But fishing fleets capture so many bluefins with their nets that only a few have time to grow into large fish.

The survival of other ocean fishes is also threatened because of overfishing. The population of Atlantic cod is just a tenth of what it was. Several kinds of sharks have nearly disappeared. Many large fishes, such as marlin and sailfish, are now hard to find.

Scientists with the World Wildlife Fund believe that the only solution to overfishing will be to place large sections of the world's oceans off limits to **commercial** fleets.

Fished for Their Fins

Sharks like this hammerhead are often caught only for their fins. The fins are used to make shark fin soup. The rest of the sharks' bodies are thrown back into the sea.

Many bluefin tuna are caught before they reach their full size.

Fast Facts About Sockeye Salmon	
Scientific name	*Oncorhynchus nerka*
Class	Actinopterygii
Order	Salmoniformes
Size	Up to 33 inches (84 cm) long
Average Weight	6 to 8 pounds (3 to 4 kg)
Top speed	About 25 miles (40 km) per hour
Habitat	Northern Pacific Ocean, rivers and lakes of northern Asia and North America

Glossary

breeding — producing young

cartilage — tough, flexible body tissue that forms the skeletons of sharks, rays, and jawless fishes

cold-blooded — having a body temperature that changes with the animal's habitat

commercial — for business or trade

coral reef — a large underwater formation created from the skeletons of coral animals

fish — one or more of the same kind (species) of fish

fishes — two or more different kinds of fishes

gill — a body part of a fish that lets it breathe underwater by transferring oxygen from the water to the fish's bloodstream

gill slits — slits on the heads of a fish through which water leaves the fish's body

lateral line — a line of nerve endings along the sides of a fish's body that detects vibrations and pressure changes in the water

oxygen — a gas in the air or in water that all living things need

predator — an animal that hunts and eats other animals to survive

prey — animals that are hunted by other animals for food

school — a group of fish swimming together

swim bladder — a sac filled with air inside many fishes that helps them change depth

taste buds — tiny nerve endings for detecting tastes

Fishes: Show What You Know

How much have you learned about fishes? Grab a piece of paper and a pencil and write your answers down.

1. What are sockeye salmon called when they first hatch?

2. What is the name of a gas that all animals need to live?

3. What are the three main groups of fishes?

4. What is the name of the sac that bony fishes use to go up or down in the water?

5. Where are fishes' ears located?

6. Why do fishes use less energy when they swim in groups?

7. What does a frogfish use to attract prey?

8. What is the name of the special pocket for eggs on the male seahorse?

9. Why do clownfish always stay close to sea anemones?

10. How many kinds of fishes have scientists identified?

1. Alevins 2. Oxygen 3. Bony fishes, sharks and rays, and jawless fishes 4. Swim bladder 5. Inside the head, behind the eyes 6. Because fishes create water currents when they swim and give a boost to the others 7. A lure above its mouth 8. Brood pouch 9. For protection, because they are not affected by their poison 10. About 25,000

For More Information

Books

Encyclopedia Prehistorica: Sharks and Other Sea Monsters. Sabuda, Robert and Reinhart, Matthew (Candlewick, 2006)

Hello, Fish! Visiting the Coral Reef. Earle, Sylvia A. (National Geographic, 2001)

How Do Fish Breathe Underwater? Tell Me Why, Tell Me How (series). Stewart, Melissa (Benchmark Books, 2006)

Web Sites

Coral Reef Conservation Program

www.coralreef.noaa.gov

Learn all about coral reefs, and find out how you can help preserve them for future generations. Follow links for games and a free coloring book.

National Geographic: Fish

www.nationalgeographic.com/animals/fish.html

Find out basic facts about all kinds of fish. Be sure to check out the colorful photos and video links.

Index